STRUCK DUMB WITH SINGING

STRUCK DUMB WITH SINGING

LeighAnna Schesser

PITTSBURGH:
Lambing Press, 2020

Acknowledgments

Grateful acknowledgment to the publications where the following poems first appeared, sometimes in slightly different forms:

"Odyssey" in *Dappled Things*, forthcoming, 2020.

"Innocence" in *Dappled Things*, forthcoming, 2020.

"Kansas in July is a State of Mind" in *Flint Hills Review*, Issue 24, 2019.

"Good Friday's A Hard Rain That Won't Fall" in *Dappled Things*, Pentecost 2018.

"The Final Boast of Love's Eternal Yearning" in *Angelus*, April 2018.

"After the Fig Leaves, Eve Cuts Her Hair" in *Presence: A Journal of Catholic Poetry*, April 2018.

"Empathy" in *Virga*, May 2017.

"Named" in *HeartWood*, April 2017.

"The Thinness of Things" in *Peacock Journal*, October 2016.

"Canticle of Philomela" in *Peacock Journal*, October 2016.

"Sacrament" in *Peacock Journal,* October 2016.

"Rising" in *Peacock Journal*, October 2016.

"Women's Work" in *Peacock Journal*, October 2016.

"Urgency" in *Heartland*, Anchor & Plume Press, 2016.

"A Time to Sow" in *Heartland*, Anchor & Plume Press, 2016.

"The Politics of Being" in *Heartland*, Anchor & Plume Press, 2016.

"Driving Out of the Flint Hills" in *Heartland*, Anchor & Plume Press, 2016.

"Rib and Marrow, Soil, Green" in *Heartland*, Anchor & Plume Press, 2016.

"The Dunes" in *Heartland*, Anchor & Plume Press, 2016.

"Love Poem" in *Heartland*, Anchor & Plume Press, 2016.

"Wheat Psalm" in *Kindred*, Fall 2015 and *Heartland,* Anchor & Plume Press, 2016.

"On the Westward Expanse" in *Heartland*, Anchor & Plume Press, 2016

"The Song of the Lark" in *Ekphrastic*, January 16, 2016.

"Baptism of the Neophytes" in *Ekphrastic*, January 16, 2016.

"Bivouacked" in *Rose Red Review*, winter 2015.

The italicized lines in "Love Poem" are quotations from the Song of Songs (RSV-2CE), except for the final italicized couplet, which borrows phrases from Jack Gilbert's poem "The Forgotten Dialect of the Heart." The title "Good Friday's A Hard Rain That Won't Fall" is a line borrowed from Charles Wright's poem "When You're Lost in Juarez, in the Rain, and It's Easter Time Too." In "Empathy," The third stanza draws from Brenda Shaughnessy's *Human Dark with Sugar* and Bonnefoy's phrase "interior sea lighted by turning eagles"; "Louise" refers to Louise Gluck's *Ararat;* the sixth stanza is a fusion of Isaiah 6:6-8 and Caedmon; "The act of the poem…" is an elaboration of a phrase from Wallace Stevens' "Modern Poetry"; and the quotation in the final stanza of is from Li-Young Lee's poem "Braiding Poem" in *Rose* (BOA, 1993).

CONTENTS

Creation Story

God delighted in feathers
so he started with a perchless ocean.

There was a thing that sang, yes,
but no soul yet to chorus in.

Hope means that which is complete
pours out abundance for what isn't.

An empty sea, a strong wind,
waves with no land to break them.

Firmament, first testament, bridged
one day by olive branch,

but not yet. The endless light
must have a where to travel,

after all, a gravity to fall
against—to flame upon the rim—

and, at last, upend. Crumbled edge,
un-native chalice, grave

love, plumed and preening
Other—the heaving spirit

pulling with the reins of wind.
Spilling heartwrench first,

breaking prism infinite
into teeming, singing matter.

Canticle of Philomela

The story that cannot be told will be.
Some silences must be signed into being,
fingers into palm, read with toes in
the lines and lumps of dark wet roots,
traced in the sky with brown feathers.

*

My royal name was Philomela
in your love poems. I burn
it in the rising darkness
I sing each night, wave
under wave, land under land.

Your love is a blind fingerprint,
grafted to each blank new face
of your selfishness.

When you come for me
with your closed, stitched mouth,
I will be harvesting olives,
I will be the nightingale, singing.

*

Makers of words, this is your lullaby.
You are begotten of words,
and begotten, you beget.

Who planted this tongued root of love,
wriggling and warm, alone in the dark?
I will harvest its heartlessness: sweet sprout
and bitter blossom, the tonguelessness of grief.

*

Sometimes, the telling burns.
Sometimes, the teller.

So be it.

After the Thanksgiving

Turtle-flipped moon, back-sprawled shell,
you are both charm and token. We carry you

forward, head-balanced, a dry bucket
towards some future, half-expected well.

In the frayed, backwards seam of the year,
we look into the long rip of mourning,

an opened ribcage in the ungrowing cold.
Light a fire. Roast our hunger for a feast.

Somewhere, charred cold beneath the
geese-tracked clouds, we are haunted

by darkening visions of a sightless sky.
What's coming, comes, again and again.

At the further end of harvest, where the
rationing begins, we submit our naked necks,

thrummed stiff with song, to the wide blue
veil, loose knit, caught with seeds of light.

Our flesh goose-pimples with the stars.
Sing a little louder, sisters, these lungs

are only bellows, the drone beneath
the sparkdark words our only heat.

Moon, open eye, rolling sleep. Haunt
of howlers, poets, appetites with fangs.

Who dark-cream floats in tree-skimmed
cup. Bright burn mark, chilled to ash

with distance from the flame—
We name you, but can't beseech what

doesn't answer. Even so. Hold us, sighted,
slow-sap pale, silver-lit. Don't blink.

Bivouacked

The secret to being a hero is accepting
the journey. You will know it by

this: it is the one you do not want to take.

*

To believe that words go back before the beginning. Come from.
That everything came from words
    (light and water, wind and dust)
but us.

And we are clay. Or little piles of ash, clinging to breath and
    currents,
reaching for words, to use and stroke, but powerless. The words
have power over us.
    Speak through us.

What is truth to speak it? What is truth that speaks?

A Word speaking words to word-makers,
    little clay dolls at their potter's wheels.

*

Sorrow is a grey mist and I am its keeper,
the crystal ball that traps it, tames it into
telling truths, a future. Always

the same one.

Sorrow folds itself like dough between
my palms, holds its breath and dives
down to rest like marrow
in my bones, to dry into ash,
then not even ash:
    the hollow after,

that rises. To make me into bird
bones, empty enough to fly, too
empty to remember to whom.

*

How do I wait? How long?
The way you wait for a loved, lost thing.

Toll

What is a bell but the burden of echo?
Announce! And tell, and tell, and tell.

The keeper, the farmer, or child who knows
carries the news to the bees: toil and knell,

honey and water, sticky and copper the sorrow
when the hive does the dance of the bell.

Tip to the ferry man, tip to the bees,
for the pole and the comb and remembering me.

Winter in a New Year

Three hay bales, one headlight.
The anonymous road, and we
who itch it, up and down compulsively.
Some unnumbered winter morning.

The gray sky is a clenched heart,
a burdened love, a burdensome love,
unpoured. A world and her lover
soaked for days in dishwasher light.

Hard to tell what inner landscape
satellites with this one. A rising
and a setting, seesaw tandem—
the tension that connects. Compels.

There are blues and there are blues.
Skies you gasp in and skies
that gasp, surflike, in you.

Water for the Journey

First I carried my hands curved like bird beaks,
little dippers searching and yearning.
But it was not enough. Beneath the starred,
restless sky, tilt-a-whirl axis and everything spills.

Then I tried my palms as wells, overlapping,
double deep, dug further and further away.
But the slippery damp of stone cannot
be climbed or carried, only coveted.

What runs upward but a river burdened
by the foresight of long sprayfall to ocean?
To struggle against the seep and leak.
Against the pull to plunge, to dissipate.

There is no bucket but these nets of hope,
raveled through two sieve-hands. The path is dry,
the chart for star-reflection only. I lay my skin
flat upon the wish of waves, and breathe.

A Time to Sow

What is it about sunflowers? Bright brown
faces too large, encircled by bent yellow
beards, I keep waiting for them to smile.

Fall comes quickly to Kansas. The sunflowers
bob their huge noses, sniffing in the first
promise of northern gales. Their stout green

bodies shiver in ditches, trimming empty fields,
thick stalks bowing south, then north, caught
between two winds in the days of sunlight

grown dim and cold. They can only watch
as the hard red wheat is sown for winter: a
promise of December snows, a someday sun.

They bow their faded heads. I wonder if they,
too, wait in joyful hope for the coming of
a peeled yellow springtime, bright as petals.

Soon, their brittle stalks will snap, land lightly
on dry soil, their broad, open faces still skyward.

Sic Transit Gloria Mundi

Where the serpent-belly of timelessness
scraped the thickening firmament,
the prairie rises. Hills creep up subtle
as bubbles in a watched kettle.
Prairie is the emptiness drawing out ours.

Grassland, uneven as weekday prayer,
lays close against the slender throat
of the waters. There is always a well,
a rope, a vessel, and what rises.

Even unevenness is patterned, steady.
Little low rivers, grasses waist-high,
hills and peaks going sharp deep,
the crust of dry soil cut away raw
to pressed red, smooth brown bone.

We who exhale over this blooming,
this headlong, this breeze-creased face,
learn bending to and bearing up,
its climbings and clamberings; broad
stooped back, miles-flattened feet.

Restlessness trails back and forth, moving across
the face of the earth. Breakers of years ascend
again and again to our lips, dripping sweet and whole
from the flung-out palms of unceasing winds.

Prairie, burn the green wick of your ground-life
as long as there are ears to hear your mouthing wind,
longer than there are eyes to run you smooth with longing,
as long as furthest, sleep-spelled end. As long as
this well, its vessel, and the rope that lowers us in.

The Politics of Being

Lightness of bread. Dew-budded dawns, clear nectar.
Aubades recited silently at dusk—anticipation. I am a clutch
of words stumbling through a universe written
in the language of textures.

The skin, love-sung.
Light, broken, confetti through streaked glass.
A struggle of songbirds in shadows, breeze-hushed.

Bitter pooling in the bottom of the sweet.
The pulsing ache of the wounded, wounding world,
opening and closing, filled and emptied,
a night-shy flower, a single lung.

Ex Nihilo

Something is chasing me across the daylight.
I dream in architecture and in monsters;
firm sense of place, furry sense of self.
Sometimes I'm my heroes, but
I don't stay heroic. Other times, I'm two
or three people, me and not-me, a chorus.

Sometimes, dreams reach out from sleep,
wrap slender fingers around my wrist.
I mean that sometimes, not asleep, my mind slips
and moves like dreams. When I notice, it breaks
their fragile grip, but I can just glimpse the shape
of the face they wore. Once it was a cube of light,
combination of lives, padlock of loss, prison of maybes.

I am afraid of how much I am not afraid.
Of the light shedding these shadows
that cling at the corners of my eyes.
Of the light that casts no shadows.
Of being in the light,
the incomprehensible light,
and it not being in me.

There was light in the beginning, it's said,
and before light, the Word, but not the word *for* light.
That came later, with us, with naming, and later still
with an exodus of knowledge of what is:
Who will I tell them sent me?

Yet the word *light* is not a name,
light remains unnamed, remains itself as it is,
leaves us rationalizing particles into waves.
There's rarely water in my dreams but waves
are everywhere, the center of everything,
the center that will hold if I have to make it hold,
have to hold it myself, in the turning, dropping dark.

I've heard that darkness moves faster than light,
is always there first, but that's wrong.
Dark doesn't travel. Dark is the womb light grows in,
darkness of the spirit of the word
moving across the face of the waters,
speaking its shining reflection into being,
making meaning into beings.

I poise the pen to make my own. I am ready to forget
how sometimes I think my dreams are making me up.
Ready to take the tongued secrets of wordlessness
by taste and touch alone. Because there is light
we have no name for, words with no names for themselves,
and sometimes, I wish I shed light as easily as shadow.

But we are only told what is, not what means.
We are left with the deciding, the speaking
you cannot speak until it speaks you.
And this is mine: I will be the wild light monster
sprinting through corridors of dreams,
will be choirs of waves colliding
with crash and spray in the dark and heart of what is,
crying and calling out, again and again, *I am, I am.*

Driving Out of the Flint Hills

The sudden clefts in the ground go straight down,
lightning-ragged paths through little leaping hills,

arroyos darting between tall swaths of prairie grasses:
Bluestem, Indian, straw-gold pale in the cold. The turnpike

rolls out ahead straight as an arrow in the wind
under bright, uniform late-winter light. The sun's

all serious business until its long fingers scrape and fist
the earth, tease and twist, playful in car windows,

scuttle dark beneath little runs of green-needle trees.
Dusty dim, white-blue horizon, pale as a face too far

from summer, never gets any nearer. Bare branches salute
us by in silence; the only wind is this old car's reedy whistle.

We wait for this wide, dry, paper strip of a road to roll up
thick behind us, parsing as we pass every distant red barn

into harvests, spring births, seeds saved, and cold,
sweet secret, half-thawed ponds. Roots grow long here,

longer than branches, like deep wells of silence
beneath a quick, just-wetted tongue.

Dialogue with a Cottonwood Tree

Sunspill, ossified, dirt-plunged. Each grain
Tilted slowly, trickling down. Drink
The sleep of earth. Breathe green. What stilled,
Climbing hunger—bent and beckoned sky.

We all begin as seed. Spilt reckless, a sowing
along an old, thin seam: the promise of another
season, the love—or duty—that means return,
renew. The obligation of continue. How often
have I sat beneath a thirsty stretch of limbs
and—anything? Prayed. Desired. Begged.
Not once. At every moment.

The sapling in my heart bends and bends
And will not break. At last, so much
Bending is a twisting, cannot be unknotted.
Where there is water, we grow thirstier still.
Light is a seeping need, a damp, fragrant greed.

We leaf and sun-spark, too, in the glimmer-
streaking waves, rays of part-time immortality.
We know we mean, the pleasure of love—
the long vernal afternoon that has no right
beginning, but is ever on the cusp of ending.
Blue-beaked world, your mate-call warble throttles
me with with unsourced singing, mock measures

of counterfeit anticipated pleasure. And then
the dark, the silence, like a bell—ringing!

    A piece of time cut short
    (Cut out) is like a living tail
    Cut loose (cut off.) A body tailless
    May live elsewhere but this string
    Of furred or feathered muscle—
    A long cord of my heart, sharp neat,
    Cylindrical, pulled out. From finest
    Root's tip to lace-feathered leaf edge:
    A trailing into nothings. I
    Am time. I start and stop. Radiant.

The ringing flowered into a green smudge
of reflection which clarified into the base
element common to sky, light, water, and
regret. I woke beneath the tree, me,
a we. Dream tree shook with laughter
and my roots crawled free. Weak, on
hands and knees, to smell the water-riven
earth. Thirsty, thirsting, thirsted tree. I
liquefy. Drink.

    Summer is no silence, but a hum:
    Wind and insects and the bone-blind
    Noise of light. I, too, am skeleton, know
    Marrow and what it is to take and
    Give. Hum, sung, riverbank stung.
    Neverlasting everness.

Tree by moonlight, mouth by noonlight.
    The weeping, leafing tongue.
To autumn, to darkrise, to riverdwindle.
    To song-sung, after; and the echo.

Perspective

We all need saving from something
sometime. Summer brews and scalds,
shallow-burnt as the last half-cup
of coffee left on past noon.

My pulse skids and gallops.
On the hot porch in the mosquito-whine night,
the cardboard jigsaw is sticky, peels like pastry.
Some things should be set but fade and fade.
And others linger.

The moon sings white noise through
clouds and light pollution. Go to bed soon,
that bladed crescent croons, you can never
choose what saves you. Only
how to carry the gift of gratitude.

Kansas in July is a State of Mind

The great rust-red bulbous heads of milo.
Vines of buffalo gourd like ponderous breasts.
The thin giraffe necks of the yucca below
wide oval faces. White yarrow, red sour dock.
Sand art layered vistas: tender spring green,
sun-bleached tan, gold smoke. Circled dust-curls
of vultures rising and falling; distant jumps
of jack rabbits like waves of blowing sand
among the wind-quivered mare's tale. The dry,
mind-blinding heat baking the inessential out of you.
A land of light, untouched by human feet.

The heat is a wide long-haired dog
on your stomach with his tongue in your face.
Lungpress, heavy handkerchief.
The endless wait.

*

At last: Rain dumps down, fat and full and fast.
At last. My dry, feathered soul perks up,
ruffles and fluffs; the beak in my chest
rises up, ready to pierce, to drink.

Good natured thunder-grumble, keep
speaking to me. Keep the long grasses
bending and dripping. Exhort the heavenly sea
to dive, dive—

Call my name across the night.
May my dreams be full of feathers and leaves
and the running, racing wet.

*

The rich silt weave of daily everything:
slow, heavy waking, drying sweat, shoulder
aches; the hiss and plump, satisfying dripples
of fresh-ground coffee liquefying into the pot.

The fat, melancholy heart, happy even its
sauce of bittersweet, roasting into heaven
a minute's hot beats at a time—too much
to love, too much to love, so much,
so worthy, to lose.

*

An hour before sunset, driving east.
Long sunlight, deepening from noon's loud
triumphant fist to the soaking, velvet honey
lapping at twilight's shore.

The wind-wavy yucca, swaying tipsy
as a wedding toast-maker,
pale swaths of dry grass, bunched
like a girl's ponytail,
a skyfull of languid gray waves,
one dark shore like smoke overhead,

the dark herons' silhouetted wings beating
like slow wide oars lowered in mist.

This is the way of love: a radiant fierceness
learning to melt and layer, wrapped and wondrous,
a long-fingered, hand-holding tenderness.

Hummingbird, Telescope

The private shyness of the flower, the petal-gap cleft,
nectar cup. Inwardness. The singular, intimate dark.
Raw light, syrup light, floating in the dusty night.

Flit whit, shutter click; beak-horn, draught-sweet. Hum-
mm. Elongate, penetrate; reach out, draw in.
The shining beak, the widening, mirrored eye.

Cooldark, deepstill, above-well, air-bone streak-stop.
Pierce deep the secret dark. Drink light.

Full Lunar Eclipse

Moonwinked, red, the shadow of Earth
passes across the sky, negative searchlight.
Luna, heavy with dark, an iris smoldering.
Cloud-clear heavens tremble in refraction,
diffraction, waver through dull light-polluted
air; constellations watermarked with Milky Way.

We have extended our sight with long glass
and mirrors, jumped into light, left dusty prints
on unearthly ground; we can name the long inner
maze-walks of all these wavering orbs, and still,
still—here, two feet heavy-set on green-grown soil,
all the wailing in my hollow ribs is more ancient,
less-named watchfulness, a seedling dark—

I am eyes-wide, night-alive, a ground-bound gravity-strung
wind gusting upward, a low, whistling gray twilight;
memory of world-ends, tide-stretched, wolf-keen.
I am land-pierced and spirit-thin as this field of foxtails.
We bristle and shiver under sky, sky, sky.

Rising

Night sky, bitten plum,
above stone-hollow mortals
grasping fragile to blue
wool star warmth, low heat
of promise, person-nearness,
in the long, darkening watch.

This godleap desire springs
firmament stars from deep
heaven furrows, bloom-
blossom bright down white
stem-trail sky-hanging,
grow, dark sea, grow,
and milky-wave reach
to earth. Touch

gently our sleeping,
flint strike, burning ice,
the vast void sail-yearning
unfurling in our old
dust, these earth-seed,
skydazed, light-rung hearts.

Acceleration

Gravity unravels
us. Pulled back far
enough, we dissolve.
We are weft-fall
through timeweave;
spacecleft. It warps,
we twist; we turn,
it curves. We are
not distinct.

If we reversed
the plunge of time,
swayed gravity's
tide, we'd unstitch
our being. Some
things, once rent,
cannot be mended.

We move only
forward, twisting
through the pull,
knitting together.

Each of us a shore,
some warm wharf,
the wind warns us
about these ropes

and broad-bellied,
sun-mirror sails.

Pulled to the sea,
the sea hauled
tideward, the wrench
of conforming, what
must be, being,
becoming.

Fear and Devotion

Dim stars illuminate just themselves.
A passion, blanched
by time is distance is depth

Is moments like marbles, star-glowed, aligned
and trembly waiting for the surface tilt,
amnesiac shine, alone, each, alone.

This is not the final word. That is later,
always; beyond endurance
is what must be endured.

Through heatless time-miles, life darkens
out of the iron. Bile and bite, the beat
inevitable, beat, the pounding

of human recognition: to call it even
where it's not. To call it human even
where it's not. Therefore to see

is to create is the kindling
of kinship awash in the spark
of want. To be is to need

and to need is to peal and to
strike, reverberate echo,
hello, hello. Burst and batter,

tideless murk murmur, my bell-mouth
wavebreaks, plummets and plants,
splintering the even shore

of memory (is hope, is faith-kept.)
Tongue-peal by lash, lash by peal,
the toll takes, and takes, is taken.

Odyssey

In the Swamp of Ugliness

If only that high, twilight hope,
shining purple stream, nebulous gauze
shot through with pearl and silver gleam,
could bind our sight evening after evening—
but no. We duck our heads, we peel and shuck
beneath a blind husk of cast-off light. The pallor,
from above, as of some lower hell. Fire
and brimstone and us below. Larval,
satisfied in our polluted nest, dulled
to longing's ache.

It Begins with the Gaze

Leaves of dreams steep in the thin waters
that carry us, cupped and half-sleeping,
through the bright open windows of our lives.
A white curtain. A relaxed hand. The yellow
wall, memory-fresh. These perfumed cups,
still steaming, set aside as if we weren't really
leaving, as if we meant, in a moment,
to come back. Never left.

The stars stir and storm above us.
We swim, darkdrunk, twilight-blossoms
tumbling beneath them, on this ancient wheel
flung reckless down the corridors of darkness.

The stars dance fitfully as we, but we
only last as long as puffs of breath
in airless space, and cannot see.

Launch At Three Million MPH

Rise, swords of desire—
unsheathe glitter-sharp. Splendor,
your name is grief of immortality.
Ambition must be gallows, if only death
is always.
        Space. Dark. Spotted with lights
like wild eyes, distant lamps, a billion shores
marked against the indigo with burning towers.

The future is the only house big enough for all
and yet it's time long passed that we sail into,
launching little boats into the rolling black,
the immense tide-drawn past, from which
even the lucky living will find there is
no ever leaving. No going back.

The First Generation Ships Raise Their Children

Space takes up residence inside of us.
A hollow seed, inverted, births the plant
with black leaves and steel-gray flowers
uncurling in our necks.

We open our mouths and stars fall out.
Hungry, hungry, in between the suns

of almost home, can't-be home, wish-was home.
We would kneel and shovel dirt
into our sun-abandoned mouths,
but in space, no gravity—no down—
no ground.

Our bones evaporate. Like mosaic windows
streamed through with radiation,
though human born, we begin to taste
a whispered name: alien.
                              Location, location.

We mouth and sign. All must be silence
in the star-reft void.

And Some of Them Believe

He who would be a priest must ask: what is bread?
The ship cannot tell him. Fire is a number
on a calculating screen. Flour is forbidden,
a loose white storm. The alchemy of heat-change
must be unknown in the metal belly
of the holding pattern—fire, after all, eats air—
must pause, to endure the long
kite-tail stream, sail-fling, shot forth
between hearths, harvests, hearts.

Someday, some inhuman ground
will be trod by merely human feet.
But there will be no fleshy God
to pluck forbidden heads of grain.

There will be no wheat.

Body of Christ, how will we survive,
where you have never been to toil, sow, and reap,
to sanctify our bodysoil?

Lazarus Waits

Every scorched and frozen rock we will
gratefully call earth. Chew our space-grown
peas, kick the lifeless dirt. And but for
waste of water, we would weep.

Here we are, Lord—buried breathless in the dark.
Call us second-life, by name, by hand
reached out for hand. Bring your tears
to us once more.

Make us breath-wet clay again,
grounded, breathing, unwrapped and blinking
in the bright tomb door.

Separation

Clocks are not the incarnation of the hour—
what can it be to slumber in one body
and wake in a new? I can't conceive of us carved free,
hollowed from these greedy selves.

Flesh, I name you: not to conjure, but to bind.
This wet earth is also root; to cut and part is always death.
Regret and sorry, weights unequal in the mind.
My love is this: I would be both the leaving, and the left.

It becomes hard to see your face, recall your hands.
When we re-new, will we still be ours?
Resurrection seems more autumnal than spring.
Beneath the stern, bright skin something more

alive than blood, more me than me, breathes,
they say, that's how it is for everyone—but none
who know are near enough to ask, or be told.
Come closer, September, my lover. Come home.

The Passing of Seasons Becomes Me

Blue breath, bumble-blown, bee-flower
fingertip. Hush gaze, dusk gray, needle-

point inhale wanting. Goose and duck,
feathered and foreign, bottom-weight clouds.

The sharp that lasts. Winter, that is, loss.
Words break like sun-sucked clay,

bone of my flesh, disintegrate. Windlorn
hope of dandelions, fumbled freedom;

crystalized pasts harden forward paths.
At the death of the year, mend and rend,

the settling sediment of eternal tasks.
We are always only ready to begin.

Named

What claw and talon beast of wonder
hunts in the hills of my heart now?
A star for a face, lion-maned,
hawk-tailed, a runner's feet and
archer's bow—a body expansive
as billows blown between suns.

Rough wind, weather me down!
Long-fingered hands, be water! Waves,
carve a gully through my rock shoulders,
sandstone belly, make me cavernous and
cathedral-grand, hollow-holy.

The long pant of noon. Twilight
star-tremolo. Join them, far-spread
hands coming together, and that
is the sky I've swallowed.

I am heavy, transparent, light-borne,
wind-drifted. A lashed raft of desires
and memories of places to call home.
Bunches of perfect peach-halves,
sweet summer hemispheres,
curled about a hard, tooth-cracking
hope for a warm-dirt banked,
fresh-rooted, ivy-trellised spring.

The Song of the Lark

After the painting by Jules Breton

Red light is a song, string solo,
fiddle melancholy; somebody's sunset
waltz tipped arrowhead, let
the shaft fly.

Dull circle plod of seasons: grow and die,
grow and dye, and, oh, you and I—

tunnel vision. Look up, sudden!
Rough-as-furrow, grabbed and shook,
hooked, look! There's

a shade of redgold sunhold
never seen. The string pricks,
the bow skips,

and here I am, come home to myself
in this stupid joy, this buzz-numb hope,
struck dumb with singing, singing.

The Final Boast of Love's Eternal Yearning
for Sharon and William

Time is full of riches in the autumn of the year,
When light is thick as honey poured and spun,
The harvest yield is only just begun,
And every step is crimson, every breath is clear.
Rivers cold with light run beside the antlered deer,
Bristled trees unsheathe their flames at once—
Summer's work re-planted, not undone—
And every star is frosted crisp and near.
The majesty of seasons is their turning,
But the splendor of the vow is ever-keeping.
Now we reach the advent of a promise,
The only easy yoke and gentle harness,
A yearning only just matured and deepened:
The hour, come at last, of the beloved.

Wheat Psalm

In the shadowsunk field, breeze-blurred wheat
weaves wavelets, river-ripples, pulses low
and songlike: *ripe, gold, ripen golden*.

Tawny suntails just touch the field's face, one
last goodnight, smooth out its unplanted, wild ragged
ditch borders. The air is yellow and earthen,

all wine and perfume, with all the green of growing.
What is this feeling that slides, sea monster-like,
beneath the currents of warm breezes?

A lithe, scaled joy, hot under hand and dark-eyed,
speaking secrets through its skin, wordless, wise.
A harvest, of a kind: seed and stalk, sky and soil,

wet and dry in cycle. A promise and its keeping.
Listen: this inner sea, bright as lion light.
Wavecrash and heartbud, open, open.

The Farmer Takes a Wife

First harvest was a heat-soaked swath of freedom.
The wheat was short and bushed as a bristle brush,
all wave and scrub. Down its curving rows, a rush
of fat late light, butter-thick; the combine's high drone,
bracing white roar; rush of joining, chink and fit,
as grass sown lightly leaps roots below, then rises.
This is the liberty of love, the privilege of planting
your feet: shiver and shine to browning, to the grind
and bake and breaking of bread. Duty belonging;
be to, be for. Become more. We, wind-listed, sun-blood
links in unfolding human generations, till and keeping
path and way atop the changeless change of motion.

Rib and Marrow, Soil, Green

I love the tall grass, its little darting paths,
sleek-combed stalks bowed sideways in the wind,
soft and trim under grey skies, long-rayed sunsets.
Your deep, easy breaths among the damp and dirt.

Light, flax and amber, laps over the dark earth, nearly
sable in its satisfaction, soaked and quenched. The little
pale stones underfoot make a muted crunching, a thick,
uneven tread, lumpy and satisfying under rubber soles.
Lazy fingers part brome and foxtail; our heads twin tilts,
waiting for the dip and trill of meadowlarks.
Still pond waterline below our feet.

Up the bank and east, corn stubble rakes rough between
rows of young wheat, thin and trembly. We walk between
the long, curved lines, counting spaces where the planter
skittered, skipped, freckling the incline. Those little blanks
play counterpoint to robins, turtle doves, their twined rising
twitters, their low lone coos.

Please: take my wavering shadow, wrap it around your
knuckles, tuck in its end with your scarred, nimble thumb.
Wind it into your warm palm and cast it out behind us,
next to yours, two narrow sails, frayed standards, rippling
side by side. Planted here, your roots are mine,
your cup my well, your till my keep.

Urgency

The urgency of roots. Of sprouting things. Of buds,
green-cupped, pink and white, and the controlled somersault
of leaping seasons. Of little wooden bridges, missing slats,
tiptoeing across tiny rivers, and anthills, dusty and eroded
in a drought, of dried-out footprints. Of the sudden scattering
of fossils, shells and clams and minuscule round segmented things,
when dirt and shoes and flailing arms break away down riverside
embankments. Of finding the bees and telling them your truths,
letting sorrow translate into honey and the low blue flightpath
of flower-riders, sweet-keepers. Of the litany of birdsongs heard
and named across a season of Sundays, the wear of good boots
down across a decade, the imperceptible flaking away
of an old barn's red paint, down to its blue-grey skeleton, contented
in its wind-rocking, ivy-trailing dotage. Of the slow growth,
slow turning-over in its sleep, of something so immense
we can't stand back far enough to see it breathe. Of the quiet
insistence, ever-present pressure, of what goes on. Of the time
it takes to read a measured line, thick paragraph like a choked-up
    throat,
persistent lump, a threatening wet behind the eyes. Of our returning
prayer for daily bread, endlessly refrained in each wandering row
of green wheat growing golden: necessity, continued breath,
the low grand labor of the living.

Sacrament

In the meadow of marriage, my thighs, two pale fawns
in silver-green, frond-heavy light. Your spine, elegant
curve, at rest; long, broad-knuckled fingers between mine.

For you, I would interpret the mysteries of turtledoves
nestled on the wire; goldfinch's yellow flash; the hawk's
abrupt, devastating dive, into clutch and brief wet red cry;
a small death, rich soil for the bursting seeds of flight.

Two field mice between wheat shoots under waxing moon;
Two bright bells buried deep in breath-drawing chests;
Two long plaits of sea-green words turning and twining together.

For you, I will spill the moonwater well,
divine the unworded oracle of coupling.
I bring a silty palmful of deep riverwater to my lips;
taste the ground of sustenance, flooded with promise.

Til Death

Two stars shiver into each other's gravity.
Like golden bells, their falling is a chime.
Circling in, alone together, near-eternity,
two orbits merge, make their own time.
If there is such a thing as fate or doom,
among the purple skies a certain way,
then ours is something we've pursued,
a chosen course among the steps of days.
All things move slower when we're together.
The kairos of marriage warms like the sun.
But there's only one thing that lasts forever,
one flesh and one hope to which we belong.
The heavy hand of time will even frost the skies.
Bright within the unconsuming fire, our love, alive.

After the Vows

Among the swinging wheat, the susurrus,
the slipping time—pebbles on a pond.
Before the sun reveals the field, wind
and water own this certain sea; the firm
potential of what is yet unseen.
We walk together, gardeners at rest.

The chill is blue and deep but lacks the bitter
edge of winter. Slender shadows tremble,
race, flit away, yet never leave their place.
Like roots into the land, sun rays pierce
the gray to drink, return the ground of life
to soil nearly spent.

Dawn's a sword to lance the heart of earth.
And we, enchanters caught enchanted,
tremble like reluctant dew before
this wide, abundant cleaving—
terrible rising, light-split duty, what
pulled and pulling gravity we choose.

Have and Hold

The quiver and the sway is pull and depth;
an arrow fleeing sky-hoped through the heft
of gravity, unraveling, a rope of self-
fulfilling need: a longing that will ripen,
plum-bruised, into having.

This desire, what flash of bliss;
smoke of heaven caught in tinted glass.
A dark so deep it's bright,
the inside out of light, what is and could
be yours that's haunted you from always—
the future ever seeded in the past,
newborn-blind and hungry.

The weight of something living in your palm.
Everything we love, we love through skin.
Light-hauled and naked through the singing sky
over and against what plunges and what pulls,
we are alone, together, and immense.

Love Poem

Fossil hunting

The cliff rises, a white cathedral, shimmering
above pavement through two o'clock sun, sharp
as the brilliance of hope. Taut, arched, you are
a bow paused in a moment of breath by rosin-dusted
strings. Your toes bend and dig into the fine grey
powder, pushing through thin gnarly roots to the thick,
packed dirt beneath. Little avalanches pour out
from underneath your soles, streams of soft soil
and stone catching in ragged sneaker seams,
jean hems. Your knees bend and brush the slope, left
hand braced, wide and flat, on a tuft of grass, face
profiled against the rock, right hand stretched up
and over, beyond your sight, into a shadowy crevice,
seeking the dark, rounded heft of a clam.

This is how I knew you first: climber of mountains,
catcher of frogs, scaler of riverbanks,
namer of snakes, birds, fish.
Long, broad thumbs gently edging mud out
of the spiraled grooves of a sharp-tipped shell,
humming *amphiscapha, meekospira,*
unintelligible syllables of an earth-swallowed past.

Who is this that looks forth like the dawn,
perfumed with myrrh and frankincense,
terrible as an army with banners?

After talking

Four a.m. in the abbey graveyard,
where priests are buried under
headstones hazy with faded names.
Stars, streaking clouds, the wet
fire of a pale moon. Here, it is easy
to intuit that nothing ever really dies.

If I could prophesy, I would say, this
is the water-light that will shine
through us. Always.

No cocks will crow, but this dewy bench will dry
when dawn reaches across the valley behind us,
a hollow green goblet of fog, to pluck the night

like a wilting violet. We have time yet.
Day will come slowly, one small yellow boat on
a sea of leaves, nesting birds, grey creeping lizards.

We will leave before the light
touches us, carry with us
a burning canticle of light and water,
flame drawn from a well, pails filled
and refilled, lifted and lifted again,
always up the hill home.

Who is this coming up from the wilderness,
leaning upon her beloved?

The river

We walk through a sound of crickets
in the warm twilight, out past street lamps'
muggy blur, leaving crumbling sidewalks
for broad, slanting stones, stepping from one
sun-warmed side to the next, following
the trail to water's edge like gangly lizards.
You hold my sandals in both hands and
tell the river's story. I set leaves and sticks
into the current, name them barges, steamboats,
pioneers. We brush aside mosquitoes, wait
for starlight, talk softly under the long, hot
blue insect song rising on the breeze. The soft,
clear water, sediment-bruised, rushes and hugs
each brown bank in turn. Wavering light sinks
like so many sleepy dragonflies beneath the waves.

The way you swing your arms, raise them
to the curving horizon, tracing turtles and ferns
in tufted clouds snagged on silhouetted treetops.

My beloved put his hand to the latch,
and my heart was thrilled within me.

The altar

Behind your head, on the eastern wall, Christ
shoulders His cross in white porcelain relief.
Behind my head, on the west, He carries it still.
We promise to carry each other.

52

Come, my beloved,
let us go forth into the fields;
let us go out early to the vineyards,

and see whether the vines have budded,
whether the grape blossoms have opened
and the pomegranates are in bloom.
There I will give you my love.

We are given a flame to drink from
and a well to carry. We burn into blossom.

Two kitchens

One is gold, a halo of morning dust caught
in the dappled dance of light through high lace curtains.
Long and draped low to wide windowsills,
they stir in little drafts and wink the day inside.
The long table slants down both sides from the middle,
an archer's heavy bow. Wine glasses brimming
with orange juice and cheap champagne slide slowly
to the edge, stop short of spilling.

The other is brown and sweet, dusted with
the fragrant ghosts of spices: tarragon, cumin,
cardamom. We sing their names into sweet
sauces and layers of vegetables: kala namak,
celery seed, garam masala; cinnamon, marjoram,
caraway. We place food before each other. We eat.

This is eternity:
the weight we choose to lift again
and again

burning through us like a wick,
beginning to end

The same water, shed and cupped.
The same flame, lit and swallowed.

Eat, oh friends, and drink;
Drink deeply, oh lovers!

The park

The flowers appear on the earth,
we hear the voice of the turtledove.
The fig tree puts forth its figs,
and the vines are in blossom.

There will never be clouds like this again.
There will always be clouds like this.

The pine-flush mountain rises distant
like a breaking humpback, swelling
green and dense under firecracker clouds.

We bring each other coins, ink, heavy books.
And silence, wrapped in the nearness of the now.

Still and blue, the evening rolls over in its sleep,
seeking other dreamers, newer days.

Arise, my love, and come away.
We hold hands. We take a gravel road home.

Canticle

I will seek you among the pale henbit and
silky aster, heavy wild indigo, the kiss-me-quick,

the quivering brown tails of june grass. I will
seek you among the wet green corn, trembling
with dew in thin dawn light, like straw,
splintering the furrowed soil.

I will love you among the tadpole streams
surfacing in burbles from the dark clay earth.
I will love you among the wheat and the flax,
the low, scuttling ferns, and the deep red mud
growing spiked, broad-leafed vines by the river.

I will give you spiced wine to drink,
the juice of my pomegranates.

I will give you fresh, pale cheese, and
the first spring shearing, heavy with lanolin.
Whole baskets of dates, ripe round berries,
peeled red oranges, apricots, almonds.

My love is a hundred pitchers of honey,
ripe barley lithe under the wind's labor.

My love is a tall white cliff above a deep river,
a wind-carried psalm of wheat-colored light.

The Infant

I lean over him in the silent dark,
bells swinging from my chest.
They have no voice but
what weeping speaks.

Greasy with sleep, I can't quite
feel my fingers, or brush the dust
of dreams aside, but I cradle
his head, lift him up.

His round belly against mine,
rising, rising, falling. Slow blink
of wide eyes. His hummingbird hands,
cupping and uncupping, flicker

above these small round flowers.
Sedately now, his fingers come together,
warp and woof, part like a seam
unstitched, bit and piece. The steady
pace of all that should be, being.

Sleep comes and stills him, leaves
fat fingers curled, two half-open as if
in blessing. Three a.m. is a dark mercy,
a round mouth's open gift.

Husband

Sometimes dark clouds eat the moon
and the stars flee too soon
leaving night defenseless as a cradle.

Sometimes howls rise like birds of prey
and fall again, sharp and gray
as ice beneath a sky unable

to weep. Sometimes the forest swallows you
and no shot sings clear and true
to reassure us in our winter-fisted cabin.

Still you are walking, walking,
and my hearthside heart is following.
Whether clouds or wolves, I haven't

lost sight of your light, north star.
You, and I know where we are.

Shore

The point of every island is the sea.
Water flows between all things,
and beneath, the land continues,
breathing deep. Our bodies

are tides love-caught in still-warm glass, prismatic, final
form of sand on fire, lightning hooked and chain-yanked lit.
No wonder we reel moondrunk between giving in
and flinging out—riptide fish, scaled and gape-mouthed,
whip past our astonished ankles, suddenly silt-less, naked
and unanchored before the eternal, unrepeated wave.

At the center of the whirlpool
is the place of mercy: eye, throat, blessed
soft-catch between the shearing
sea-sky-sea and drowned-sleep depths.

Maelstrom minds; clear cupped chests; heaving breath.
Stop-motion wave, frantic crest-top balancing—
each smiling, beach-lazed face a wreck of starfish
just beneath. Waterwish, hung on tides outgoing: bring
us currents we can feel, sunlit, above the whirl of unknown
deep. The tug of life at other end: bring us
other dreamers in our anchored, wave-pitched sleep.

The Thinness of Things

Winter dawns with their eggshell light
and pale, spare clouds combed over a bald sky;
translucent red-peach shell of the boy's small ear;
skim of milk on day-old coffee, forgotten high
on cluttered bookshelf; time's uneven crust over old griefs,
stretched taut in fitful sleep; that harpoon leap
of ringing terror in the wool-gray night when the other car
looms, engulfs, and somehow, misses—
passes by in hollow, vacuum-hush of air, the cold release of limp
    relief—

the walls in that first apartment, amplifying every step and door,
thunk and thud, flattening, filtering, funneling voices;
flour dusted on the wooden bread board, streaks of white, stiff
    drops of oil;
film of steam on bathroom mirrors, blurring every imperfection
into smoke, amorphous shadow; how the weary blood
slows after so many late, solitary nights—

the edge between now and next, this time of year, with its dry cold,
its motley leaves, blanching into thirst for snow; hopes for
    everlastingness
strung like beads on knotted prayer cords, binding our own chill
hands to the bony wrists of every one who's already pulled aside
the last, diaphanous curtain, and, exhaling, passed—

where midnight presses against midnight, faded nearly through,
where a single finger can trace the fraying line
where walls between worlds have rubbed together,
worn and worn away to a single, cleaving shine.

Petrichor

In Memoriam Mary Oliver

We quicken in the waters with the dark still song
of the deep ground already calling in us.
Gravity anchors the womb to the grave.

Our beginning melts like a flood of spring snow.
Hawks circle above apple blossoms, bright
needles in and out above the willows.

We spend our years following after the rains,
drying out steadily as tilled soil.
The calling sinks deeper, into bone,

and at last this brittle husk crumbles
and all we are beneath, so much groundwater,
rushes away. But water is never lost,

or unmade, though lost from sight. Sink and seep,
to wait, to fertilize, to grow. A sea in the night,
a dark light, on the blue floor of eternity.

This is the way love has passed here:
we felt the flutter of its wings, the tiny chirrups
of its heart, the fresh mist of its breath.

Hills follow upon hills, blue sweeps after blue.
The earth, dry in the fields; earth, steaming after rain;
earth, singing in the clay of our flesh.

The earth has claimed you.
We claim the earth.

Recoil

In Scripture, the word recoil "expresses a total collapse: not one stone remains upon another. The same word is applied to the havoc wrought by love in God's Heart in favor of his people."
    —Pope Benedict XVI, *Behold the Pierced One* (Ignatius, 1986)

A precious stone, lost again and again in the waves:
so the days become years. Motherhood
is the grief that wounds like joy, unhealing,
unhealable. Unbearable, and borne.

Not so much born as wing-flung, soared;
not so much grown as built, clay-ground up;
air, earth, and drenched-heat forged.

The days slip by like gusts of wet wind,
breathless-damp and cold at the end,
prerequisite for the hearth-heat of embrace.

Time is a toothed fish that snaps and cuts away,
leaving absence in its wake.
These waters will never be still again.
Longing is what makes and unmakes.

Mother-love is a hunger,
marrow-deep shudder, a terrible yearn.
Most awful of awes.

And yet—God! Unbegun family,

Who hurts and doesn't hurt,
weeps and doesn't need,
dies and isn't dead.
Who fathers love and labors like a mother.
What abundant joy. What bottomless grief.

Upon what is an anvil forged?
What heft can bear, can form,
the densest of forces, the burden
of density, pained and praising,
shaped once, then ever-shaping?

My daughter, my daughters, you
are only and always your own:
in the pit of me, your own need,
your own speared, blade-flash
potency, a womb-close hollow,
capacity for rejoicing—
the grief that sings—
to be, and being, enflesh.
One way or another,

fresh fire chafes the metal, steam scorches,
endurance tempers and centers.
There is no iron like that begotten of iron,
generation unto generation,
no mother-woman like a girl, come whole
and infant-wailing into the flood,
this tremendous, ringing tenderness,
the spine-grip rage of love.

Women's Work

We prepare the living and the dead. In the heat
of daily fires we wear memory smooth,
as tight-woven wool shines to translucence
from hand to younger hand. Hush, hush, we say,
and rock the cry, one constellated star
at a time. We pull tight the knotted line, hand
over hand, enflesh the bones of time
as potters shape and break: vessels carried
and carrying towards final, dusk-musk doorway.

In Egypt, we bared and beat our breasts
through streets, became drums of absence,
the rhythm of gone-ness. In Jerusalem,
anointed the Anointed One, myrrh and aloe,
shroud-wrapped all our hopes, sealed up the kingdom
of heaven in dry stone. In Greece, opened blue
and breathless lips to weight the tongue
with ferry fee, and afterwards, washed
all the restless living with all their worldly goods.
Bleed out and purify, sacred mingling.

Always, the water divide. Living and taken,
borne and bearing; sail-still harbor of death,
whispering line between two shores, never touch.
We, ferryman's handmaidens, put feet to each bank.
We, wells and buckets by turns, raise and drop
the buzz and pull of waterfalling gravity.

We who swim as waves from tide to tide
bleed long and heavy, wrench and bucket,
years of blood in the middle of our lives.
Conduit, flash and tinder, call, response.
Blood is the life, but this flood, its absence,
its someday-ness, its lightning-ready strike
of origins—divine fingerprint.

Blood-born, moonleash led, we feel our way along
the viscous river bottom to froth and tideshore.
The pull of seaweed veins turning and twisting
inside us. Flush and wash: the weight
and dragging pull of origins against the clear dark
of oceanic singularity, drawing, again and again,
all things to itself. The crush of weight and pull
apart, sticky tear and press, deep, we're earth
leavened into bread and knuckle-kneaded
in the bent-over, long wet blur of enduring.
We, light-driven rushes of weight swung low
and lower in widening hips, redmoon-kissed,
pressed slowly below the floor with the clutch
and grunt of cost—terrible beauty, awful wound,
in the full, waxing light of a free doom.

Surrender to the need to utterly succumb.
The shadow of life passes over us; mark your
doorposts, ladies. The angel of death
is mother-red, and weeping, comes.

After the Fig Leaves, Eve Cuts Her Hair

So when they bury Abel, there is no veil
between her grief and her love. And there he stands,
so like his father, his cities yet unbuilt.

His father cuts open earth with bare hands,
leaving plough and shovel, the sharp edges
and the heavy handles, apart in furrowed field.
She calls each animal he resembles: mole, badger, fox.
He named them, once, and now she names him:
father unfathered, sonless, one son less. The sun hangs
round and clear, apple-red, above the dark tree line.

Once, when Cain was the only child in the world,
their fields withered and arrows flew fruitless.
Dull-eyed by the empty fire, beside the windless cedars,
he wailed at the dry breast. Much later,
after thunder dumbed the stars,
they faced the barren, muddied vale together. Adam said,
God made paradise, and we made this -
this is all we have to give him. He struck his staff
upon the seedless ground. Cain made two tiny fists.

Abel she cannot unsee as a splintered spear
of red lightning, reduced to kindling
on the perfumed grass, the churned earth
weeping red mud. Loss escapes her in a hiss
of distant fear: this time, the choice
for death has been made for her,

despite that it was life she'd sent into the world.
Her voiceless throat swells tight, dry as scales.

Her hair is short and stiff and gray. The world is young.
There will yet be other sons, and daughters more;
the seed of man must multiply. But this grief is older
than she knows, its gaze fixed far ahead
on what, someday, must be done. The wind's voice
keens a long lament, a parent loss,
the form of sons' deaths yet to come.

The Flesh Goes Deep

Sprung like a deer
into short skybound height,
one spindle-legged bundle
of timorous hope
at a time. Mothersigh, it isn't
only the innocent
fleeing, the doe-eyed,
weaponless, who can't protect
their downy nurslings,
all tender lips and dainty feet.

What hoofs. What teeth.
What cloven hearts
riven, rivening, beneath.

The Guilty

The way a freezing mist falls
suddenly, numbs hands and feet,
coalesces crystalline in lungs
afraid, yet yearning, for melt-shock.
Icy runwater, a kind of spring. Stunned,
and yet we walk and breathe—burning,
deep beneath the skin, just
hot enough to grieve. Like stars,

mercy's many burnpoints
are often daylight-bled away.
But they endure—and pierce us in
any sudden dark, like all
once-forgotten phoenix fires
tempered in an iron forge.

Talisman, mercy works only on the guilty.
There's nothing convenient to forgetting;
unseen is not *erased*. Better to
wash away, but remember. No such
thing as undone for the timeborn; not
even for the Unbegun.

Best to dry, driftwood-like, into fodder
for the altar-eating fire: sacrifice,
a killing that gives life. All our oaths
of would-have-it-be kindled

into offering. Always the verb,
impassioned, motion-violent. Just so,

desperation is another kind of prayer, yes,
in foment, supplication disinherited,
anger begetting pleading. An end
that continues, again and again, reborn.

Forgiveness is what's left of grief
sieved through another. Mercy-felled,
we carry our sword-pierced hearts
up the hill in vinegar hands. Having died,
we are dying. Beggared, can begin
to beg, to shrive.

The Purpose of the Incarnation

Gravity's maker, spinner of spheres and spiraling matter,
made into weight, to sweat. His own feet vulnerable,
drawn flat and close against the punishing ground.

Star-strayed infant, wrapped in weight, heavy heaven.
In the hollow of the years, long and narrow as a well,
he waits suspended, bucket-drawn, clapper in a bell.

Ringing and ringing in heatfolds of gravity, lines and lines
of weight leaning us into each other, caught up, tumbled,
open-face roses in a blue bolt of thorn-pricked cloth.

God made known, fleshly God, Godlight bodied, bleeding
out into wood, over stone. God from God, telluric God,
shadowcast God, lightstricken God, bloodwritten. The pull

electric of low, deep center. God flesh, corpus God, Verbum
corpse, light-riven. Inscribed, blooded, God-heft falling death-
bitten into weighted rising, made and given; the miracle of leaven.

Baptism of the Neophytes
After the painting by Masaccio

Weight of water, heavy as light:
as if light, liquefied, tear-streamed
down his face, made his knees
two pale fishes. Head submissive,
hair a net awash with weighted light,
the way it seems to travel both over
and through, water on and in, merging
and drenching, seen and unseen, Holy Ghost
embracing the adopted son.

What is wet is alive—thirst, primordial birth.
Our cups runneth over. The mirroring face
of the waters, eye of the world, breath-fogged,
Spirit-breathed. Void and firmament,
chalice on a stem. To ripple the still surface
of substance seeming solid, but with infinite give.

Novice, naked and neck-bowed, be submerged
in the grave of the Christ, receive his blood,
blood-brotherhood, blood washing away blood-
guilt. Enter the floodwaters in the gut
of the Ark. Be born eternal in a second womb-
water. Harbor the bloodbeating heart, the heat,
holy, holy—drink it down like water-mixed wine.
Wine was water, once, and was made new.
So you. Hold your finite breath—dive deep.

Good Friday's A Hard Rain That Won't Fall

after Charles Wright

When your gravity fails
you spin and spin out and spin
into clay-crack fracture

lightning; the open
sundering, the veil

torn, guttered and grappling
in the wind who
ravaged the cedars.

Tongueless, grief paces among
the bellflowers' violet flutes.

Holy Saturday is a bell
on the earth, round lips to the ground,
dampened in rain-mute soil.

Strong as Death
Song of Songs 8:6

On our street, a flock of vultures engulfs
the pink-splayed sunset. Feathered cloud, loud
smoke, coupled. The birds of death mate for life.

Before I was a wife, I was a jury-hung
field of clicks and whistles, negative

charge, positive pull. Love consumes.
Ever-eager for hunger. Gut-deep
call to what sustains, fulfills, renews.

We, also, are born into long dyings. To mate
for life is to mate for death: a certainty

of the singular always, that which lasts.
Pairs of hulking birds bound into grace
-fulness, flight, ensure what remains

on earth lives on in others. Temporal
immortality: nothing ever truly lost.

Marriage is apiece-ness shared, one made two,
made one and many. A reconciliation. We hold
hands beside the vulture tree, black against the sun.

Hunting for Moss Opal
Gove County, Kansas

Land, exsanguinated: dust and haze dry-boiled.
Baked blind, we feel our melted-rubber way
into the red and yellow waste. Drive slow,
and these gravel roads reveal a braille echo,
land's life jolting up between our toes.

After time, gravel becomes sand. We circle and circle,
kick up comet tails of dust. The belly of the road
is lower than the ground, deep impressed, straight
as map-marks. Any marks. We're not lost, exactly,
but can't find the right x. Deep in coffee-stained
creases the small, smudged cross calls us, patient
graphite beacon, but the earth won't line up.

We pause by a bank with a hole in it. Absent animals,
dried-out fence posts. Distant, disinterested clouds, radiating
innocence in white fleece. Loose-hung barbed wire like
ley lines, glint and glare, gleam and glimpse, puckers of sweat,
sutures of sun on rough mid-morning's upturned chin.

Two packed sand paths meet and split: crossroads
cruciform, cured solid, polish-shined with grit and light.
At last: our yearned-for ditch. Dig here, buried treasure!
One more roadside, a thousand like it elsewhere. Except -

Peel back the glaze of blind light, focus small,
in our bodies' own shadows, and see: Breadth, broken
by tiny hollows. Nuances of yellow, defiant dark greens.

Scrubbed-out horizon capped by high-flared blue. Butterscotch,

milk and caramel; soft black veins, flecked and spreading;
smooth sheen, glossed and silky, set deep, stretched long,
in tan, sun-fired Ogallala rock. Bands of moss opal,
spread wide like woven bracelets, deceptively soft,
jewel-face up, fixed firm as a sand-stuck beach-goer.

Twenty million years beneath our feet. Younger
than dinosaurs, older than our oldest ancestors,
exposed on the bright tilting saucer of the high plains,
draped over and mingled with tanned, tumbled rocks, ripe
for chisel's pick and scrape, fingers' pluck and scrabble.

We are dowsers of the creeping dendrite, gem-whisperers,
stone-diviners, patient and searching as the sun.
One tap, two taps, three, rock hammers prick seams
in the fabric of the past. We fill our cans with palm-fit
history and retreat into the air-conditioned van,
drive dustily away with our spoil, time-borrowed loot.

Sweat-stench and harsh plains edges take a long time to fade.
Eventually, the crucible of the present gives way to memory,
its kind, steady grind, the mortar and pestle of meaning-making.
In the evening, by the fire, the once-full moon thinning fast
as summer fog, I look into his eyes, and suddenly, see it:
the green and hazel prairie in its concentric circles, dendrite blacks,
flecks of golden sun - the upturned palms of this earth in
infinite act of thanksgiving, a shimmering, opalescent gratitude.

Blueshift

"The fear peculiar to man cannot be overcome by reason, but only by the presence of someone who loves him."

—Pope Benedict XVI, "Difficulties with the Apostles' Creed" in *Fundamental Speeches from Five Decades* (Ignatius, 2012)

The room is vast and strange in the near-dark and he cries,
awake in sudden night, alone with far, dim light.
What heat of presence a name invokes: *Mama*, meaning,
stay, meaning, *be light*, meaning, *lay my heartbeating*
on your heartbeating. Curl and curve of space,
distinguished spaces interlocked in link and ache,
together and not, apart and one, a falling dance, a leaning-in.
Be the inhabitation, you, the inhabiting, you, the space inhabited.
Our time under one another's hearts is short, at first sigh,
until years grow long as water between earth-curved tides.
Shadows tremble here, move like water caught on hems.
As stars pull their light like nets behind them
and all of space is sunk and shifted, blue to blue,
so the weight of you, towards me, towards you.

In the Sorrowdark

We love it because it cannot last. The wild sunflower, iris to iris
with cobalt sky; prickly goldenrod, summer's last fist-flung

laughter, petal scattered; all the yellow that must mellow,
muddle into ruddy gold; the leaves that pale to watercolor mint

beneath transparent light. Yellow is a telegram: Winter is coming,
   stop.
Kick up your heavy heels, breathe deep the leather and musk,

shake out sprightly table runners, savor sweet linen, run fleece
weighted with lanolin run over rough fingers. Where is the change,

the loss that is its own becoming? In the breath and the blood-flow
that gives the breath body, and the body, breath. The body that
   shapes

the breath touches fire to cold: hammer and smelt, hammer and
   sweat,
the sword of the years and the iron box, gently wrought, we keep

its trimmings in. Rinse me through with shivers,
I am not lost. The touchstone is warm in my pocket.

What *is* blurs into what *is not*, arrived and journey both at once,
fire circle-tamed but wild-high. Dart, shadow-quivers, between

jumping-bean flames, be caught and laugh it off, be never caught,

laugh it through, too. The trees are leaf-lost, prickle into green
   needles,

a landscape transformed, blending water and oil, kernel and husk
grown together, shelled and returned to the earth. Like a tablecloth

tucked and folded, parchment letter's wax seal new-opened,
hearth-bound embers banked and flaking to comfortable ash.

My lungs, two storms of larks, this heart in me, river-wound,
a valley full of sweet longing in the sorrowdark twilight of the year.

The Dunes
Reno County, Kansas

The ice has long retreated,
and the green-grey ocean.
When they passed, land rushed
back, alive and broken.

As if an hourglass tipped,
and stopped: those plumes
of sand are these hills,
caught and rooted,

knotted in the green and
blues and brown fruits of
spring, lavender fields
under endless sun.

Poppy-mallow blooms
thin and purple among
the calls of chorus frogs,
orioles, mourning doves.

Dipping to the ground, the heavy,
sunstar heads of Goatsbeard
lean past nodding Lady's Tresses.
Beneath, the hills break westward,

exhale the rising summer like
a lover's breath, warm

on the neck, and tumble
like golden summer storms.

Grasses taller than horses wind
upward, wave from sky to sky.
The land remembers motion,
the madness of the fall and rise,

yearns for swell and salt.
The stilled dunes, buried in
roots, curve like horses' haunches
launching for the grey horizon.

As if water, once, learned
how to die, and lying
down, flowered.

Chaplet

Never in our lives have we traveled in straight lines.
The heavens, in their concentric curves, turn
and plunge ecstatic through the flooding night;
our ground, too, whirling down the long dark waves,
one sun flared, full-sail. And we,

spun and spinning, bloomed and blushed
red and brown as autumn prairie,
are rolled thin as pastry, near-transparent,
sticky with sleep-yearning. The body
undisciplined shot through with our expansive spirits,
benevolent-fat as the wide, sleek bear.

A bouquet of starlings bursts apart, flurry of petals.
Wild sunflowers, summer's dark eyes, closed
and lashless against the rising tide of cold.
Geese blow and blare their paths between
the gray and thinning clouds.

Finger to tongue to wind:
this is where the year bends
back upon itself, circled and doubled,
wreath-wound. Shadows slivered
with pale-green light, fog-sifted light,
elm-snared light—autumn settles
on the grasses, straw-pale rose,
wilting-sun gold.

This is where we lean into the curve:
a symmetry of trees crest the hill,
rising meek and lean against
the hard blue slope. Hill and sky,
soybeans yellow as a wedding band,
cloud and clod, grass and red-tailed hawk -
garland twined and hung from palm
to palm. Hands meeting, clasped.

Innocence

My eldest daughter gives me a stick,
says, "This is your poem now."

The water at the bottom of the well shines
dark as a new moon.

Trees obscure the stars and I forget
how an afternoon of lightness
in a cotton summer blows me sail-like
over the daily surf that smooths
and mars, smooths and mars.

The stick is gray, irregular, long, light.
Now a sword, a wand, a beaten song.
Now an earth-driven staff. What will endure.

Theodicy

The sword of joy shivers us through
in the long dark well-hollow

of our loneliness. A sound like a bell.
The whole whale-weight of longing

bends, bows, breaks us asunder.
Noonlight is unrelieved justice;

shadows try to shrive us, whisper earthen
sanctity. But it's a hard light you see,

see by, prism-like, and the soft
that blinds. Seasons wash in

and out of here like tides, strike us,
long round tongues, again and against

our bell-wrung weariness. What rises, strikes—
and falls away into echo, the raw sea

surrendering another surge
to the shore-crash shattering

all swells. The land is only as still
and stable as to surfers is the crested wave,

sides sliding fall. Waveflesh,
incarnate impermanence, we are pierced

to the core, by a rapier
of holy, holy.

On the Westward Expanse

Gove County, Kansas

High plains: cloud-shade and sunspray.
A man can breathe up here, if the vastness
doesn't squeeze him. Woman, too: woman
with her man, two driftwood souls alone under
the sky's dry, cupped palm, cracked with clouds.

We are two matches tensing against open rock,
begging the wind to make our bones echo
with this dry, slumbering earth the way
seashells whistle back at ocean waves.

We are children of privilege, not pioneers, have
neither conquered nor subdued. We offer the beat
in our veins, our open fingers, to the daisy-faced
horizon, the caramel soil, for taming.

Rosewater light at sunset moistens a sea of wheat.
Love makes us transparent, sky-weathered—
a shimmer, like something bright and feathered singing
low in its throat. The land goes deep. We are free.

What We Wait For

The earth is full of quiet abundance.
Unnamed rabbits, hosts of leaves
that bud, bloom, and break unseen.
The long, hours-heavy breath of whales.
How the teeming rains sigh until
sunlight's heavy hand rests upon them.

What we wouldn't give to lay our heads
on God's beating breast
and rest in certainty.

To accept each sprouting green
without craving more, or less.

And such gifts as we daily carry home—
quietness, and breath.
                        Before and after
evening: starlight, sun. One day.
Small and silent deeds that fruit and yield.
Another day.
                Season begetting season.

Empathy

It's easier to start with what's not true.
The truth is harder because,
even when objective,
is no object, defies correlatives.
Mountains in the mind remain
unthawed by summer days—
some high countries never clear from haze.

But, perhaps, like other fictions,
(dreams, poems, winter evenings)
these lies, too, will add up
to something worth believing,

To taste about for human dark
and seek for sugar, melting hot.
To look for my own dark sea,
interior, eagle-lighted.
Though French remains beyond me,
and its poets—well, I'm trapped
beyond their burning, moonlight reach.

————

God, I miss the snow. I want to fold
its smooth, blue, midnight sheen,
as under moons, into my skin.
Not unlike Louise, who bound

her poems at the wrists
and drove snow's blinding sheets,
so many nails, into their hands and feet.

Brenda threw out the word snow, scrubbed
its footprints from her tongue, so I snatched
it up, because sometimes I still can't tell
the difference between fear and pleasure, because
I desire to be gloveless, because I thrill
to the sick plunge of temperature meeting
hot blood, tingling pulse in throbbing thumbs.

————

We all burn, beneath the snow.

Even God burns with us,
buried under, like grass bent
beneath the sleeping storm.
How long until one of us will say,
hey, we're not the only ones in pain.

————

Once, a seraph came to me, and at arm's length
he held a live coal, taken with tongs from the altar,
because not even poets, not even muses of poets,
may touch the living word and see;
not even Moses saw the face of God and lived.

And he touched my mouth with the slow, slick flame,
and said: Behold, this hath touched thy lips,
and thy iniquities shall be branded away,
and you, pitiful fortunate, will prophesy.

And I saw that it had burnt my mouth open, dark open,
and I tasted the goodness of the Lord.

And I heard the voice of the Lord, saying,
Who shall sing for me? Someone, sing;
sing me, someone, something.

And I heard my own voice, saying, Here am I, Lord, but
I do not know the song. And lo, the voice of the Lord said

———

Prophecy: the beginnings of uncreated things, the endings of
    creation.
The bitter coal and the burning scroll, honeyed mouth and bitter
    belly,
and the weight of the snow that banks it, blankets, blows.
The dark and unendurable blood. Sing.

———

What colors soak best into snow? Ochre, moonlight?
Darkening pink? Which snow soaks best into
skin? Snow you grieve through, snow erasing
stars, snow that follows you home?

When I have been cold long enough I will not remember
anymore if there is a difference between blood and snow.

When I dream of Rilke, he tells me, be
a tree in the snow. And then I am the tree
the carpenter nailed to, I am the flame of the sun
that goes out.

———————

It's taken all week to get this far, to say this much.
But here I am, at a truth: Thursdays are luminous,
filled with hazy visions. I chant *water, wedding, kingdom*;
remain bound at the wrists by wooden promises
and prophecies; chant *light, body, blood*; and the
scent of wood, cold like midnight, dry, waiting to burn.

And it is not enough, of course, but it is
the act of the poem, the mind in the prayer
of finding, the act of the prayer deciding, the hope
of the prayer in the breath of the mind becoming.

To be is to be a becoming, beloved. "And though
what's made does not abide," we live. We live.

Lightning Source UK Ltd.
Milton Keynes UK
UKHW011232260520
363905UK00002B/338